S.

D1554221

On the Na

On the
Names-of-the-Father

Jacques Lacan

Translated by Bruce Fink

polity

First published in French as *Des Noms-du-Père* © Editions du Seuil, 2005

This English edition © Polity Press, 2013

Polity Press
65 Bridge Street
Cambridge CB2 1UR, UK

Polity Press
350 Main Street
Malden, MA 02148, USA

ISBN-13: 978-0-7456-5991-6
ISBN-13: 978-0-7456-5992-3 (pb)

A catalogue record for this book is available from the British Library.

Typeset in 12.5 on 15 pt Adobe Garamond by
Servis Filmsetting Ltd, Stockport, Cheshire
Printed and bound by Clays Ltd, St Ives plc

The publisher has used its best endeavours to ensure that the URLs for external websites referred to in this book are correct and active at the time of going to press. However, the publisher has no responsibility for the websites and can make no guarantee that a site will remain live or that the content is or will remain appropriate.

Every effort has been made to trace all copyright holders, but if any have been inadvertently overlooked the publisher will be pleased to include any necessary credits in any subsequent reprint or edition.

For further information on Polity, visit our website: www.politybooks.com

Contents

Foreword

This volume brings together, not fortuitously, two talks Lacan gave ten years apart, on July 8, 1953, and November 20, 1963, on what were ostensibly very different topics.

He spoke on "The Symbolic, the Imaginary, and the Real" immediately before writing the so-called Rome Report on "The Function and Field of Speech and Language in Psychoanalysis" during the summer of 1953, a paper that marked the public debut of "Lacan's teaching," as it was later called. The earlier talk included the first thematic presentation of the famous triad that undergirded all of Lacan's work for the next three decades and that went on to become its essential object – not merely a conceptual object, but a mathematical and material one as well in the form of the Borromean knot and its derivatives.

The next talk included in this volume is the first and only class Lacan gave of his Seminar "On the Names-of-the-Father." Dramatically interrupted by Lacan's demotion from the rank of *didacticien* (which at the time meant a psychoanalyst authorized to train other psychoanalysts [i.e., a "training analyst"]), his Seminar began anew in January 1964 in the rue d'Ulm at the École Normale Supérieure with a new title: "The Four Fundamental Concepts of Psychoanalysis."

Lacan always refused to revisit the theme of the Seminar that was cut short and even to publish while he was alive the text of the single class he had given. Having concluded from his tribulations that "psychoanalytic discourse" had not authorized him to lift, as he had intended, the veil Freud had cast over the true mainspring of psychoanalysis, and that he had been struck down for his sacrilegious act, he signaled, in a word to the wise, in particular in the ironic title that he gave a later Seminar, *Les non-dupes errent*, that he would keep close to his chest truths that were too tempestuous.

The calling into question of the limits of the

Oedipus complex and of the paternal myth continued more discreetly through his seminars and writings nevertheless, going so far as to reduce the Name-of-the-Father to the level of a symptom and utensil (see the Seminar entitled *Le sinthome*, published in 2005).

The co-publication of these two talks is certainly justifiable from an historical perspective (see the bio-bibliographical indications at the end of this volume). But the true reason that I decided to bring them together lies elsewhere: to take seriously Lacan's indication in his final teaching – half-joke and half-sentence, in his classic half-speaking [*mi-dire*] way – that the symbolic, imaginary, and real are the true Names-of-the-Father.

Jacques-Alain Miller

The Symbolic, the Imaginary, and the Real

My friends, you can see that, for the first so-called scientific presentation of our new Society, I have selected a title that is quite ambitious.

I will thus begin first by apologizing for it, asking you to consider this presentation both as a summary of viewpoints that those here who are my students know well, with which they have become familiar over the past two years through my teaching, and also as a sort of preface or introduction to a certain orientation for studying psychoanalysis.

Indeed, I believe that the return to Freud's texts which my teaching has focused on for the past two years has convinced me – or rather us, all of us who have worked together – that there is no firmer grasp on human reality than that provided by Freudian psychoanalysis and that one must return to the source and apprehend, in every sense of the word, these texts.

One cannot escape the conclusion that psychoanalytic theory, and at the same time its technique, which form but one and the same thing, have undergone a sort of shrinkage and, to be quite frank, decay. For, in effect, it is not easy to remain at the level of such fullness.

Take, for example, a text like that of the Wolf

Man [*The History of an Infantile Neurosis* (1918), SE XVII]. I thought of taking it this evening as a basis for and as an example of what I wish to present to you. But although I gave a Seminar on it last year, I spent the entire day yesterday rereading the case and quite simply had the feeling that it was impossible to give you even an approximate idea of it here and that there was but one thing to be done – to give last year's Seminar again next year.

Indeed, what I perceived in this incredible text, after the work and progress we made this year on the case of the Rat Man [*Notes Upon a Case of Obsessional Neurosis* (1909), SE X], leads me to think that what I stressed last year as the crux, example, or typically characteristic thought furnished by this extraordinary text was but a simple "approach," as the Anglo-Saxons say – in other words, a first step. The upshot being that this evening I will merely try to compare and contrast briefly the three quite distinct registers that are essential registers of human reality: the symbolic, the imaginary, and the real.

I

One thing cannot escape us at the outset — namely, that there is in analysis a whole portion of our subjects' reality [*réel*] that escapes us. It did not escape Freud when he was dealing with each of his patients, but, of course, it was just as thoroughly beyond his grasp and scope.

We should be struck by the way in which he speaks of the Rat Man, setting him apart from his other patients. He concludes that he can see in him the personality of a "fine, intelligent, and cultured man," and he contrasts him with other patients he has worked with. This is not so much the case when he speaks of the Wolf Man, but he mentions it nevertheless. Still, we are not required to endorse all of his appraisals. The Wolf Man does not seem to have had quite as much class as the Rat Man. Yet it is striking that Freud singled him out as a special case. Not to mention Dora, about whom we can virtually say that he loved her.

This direct element, whereby Freud weighs and appraises personalities, cannot fail to strike us. It is something that we deal with all the time in the register of morbidity, on the one hand, and even in the register of psychoanalytic practice, with subjects who do not fall completely into the morbid category. It is an element that we must always reserve judgment about and that is especially prominent to those of us who bear the heavy burden of choosing among those who wish to go into analysis in order to undergo training as analysts.

What can we say in the end, after our selection has been made? Consider the criteria that are mentioned – must someone be neurotic in order to be a good analyst? A little bit neurotic? Highly neurotic? Certainly not, but what about not at all neurotic? In the final reckoning, is this what guides us in a judgment that no text can define and which leads us to appraise personal qualities? In other words, do we rely on the reality expressed by the following – that a subject either has the right stuff or he doesn't, that he is, as the Chinese say, *xian da*, a worthy man, or, *xiao ren*, an unworthy man? This is certainly something that constitutes the limits of our experience.

What is brought into play in analysis? Is it a real relation to the subject, namely, to recognize his reality in a certain way and according to our own measures? Is that what we deal with in analysis? Certainly not – it is indisputably something else. This is a question we ask ourselves all the time, and that is raised by all those who try to formulate a theory of psychoanalytic practice [*expérience*]. What is this practice, which is so different from all others and brings about such profound transformations in people? What are those transformations? What is their mainspring?

For years the development of psychoanalytic theory has been designed to answer this question. The average person or man in the street does not seem terribly astonished by the effectiveness of this practice that occurs entirely through speech. And he is, in the end, quite right, for indeed it works, and it would seem that, in order to explain it, we need first but demonstrate its movement by working. To speak is already to go to the heart of psychoanalytic experience. Here it makes sense to first raise a question: What is speech? In other words, what are symbols?

In truth, we witness an avoidance of this question. And we note that in minimizing this question – in seeing in the strictly technical elements and mainsprings of analysis nothing more than instruments designed to modify, through a series of successive approximations, the subject's behaviors and habits – we are led very quickly to a number of difficulties and dead ends. Going in this direction, we certainly don't go to the point of situating them in a global consideration of psychoanalytic practice, but we go ever further toward a certain number of opacities that arise and that then tend to turn analysis into a practice that seems far more irrational than it really is.

It is striking to see how many subjects who have recently engaged in analysis have talked, in their first way of expressing themselves regarding their experience, about its possibly irrational character, whereas it seems, on the contrary, that there is perhaps no more transparent technique around.

Of course, in an analysis everything goes in this direction: we fall in with a certain number of the patient's more or less partial psychological views, we speak about magical thinking, we speak about all kinds of registers that indisputably have their value and are encountered in a very dynamic fashion in psychoanalysis. There is but one step from that to thinking that psychoanalysis itself operates in the register of magical thinking, and this step is quickly taken when one does not decide first to raise the primordial question: What does the experience of speaking involve? What is the essence and exchange of speech? And to raise at the same time the question of psychoanalytic practice [*expérience*].

Let us begin with this practice as it is initially presented to us in the first theories of analysis. What is this *neurotic* whom we deal with in psychoanalysis? What is going to happen during the analysis? What about the shift [in focus] from the conscious to the unconscious? What are the forces that give a certain existence to the equilibrium we call the pleasure principle?

To proceed quickly, I will say with Raymond de Saussure that the subject hallucinates his world. The subject's illusory satisfactions are obviously of a different order than the satisfactions that find their object purely and simply in reality [*réel*]. A symptom has never sated hunger or slaked thirst in a lasting manner, unless accompanied by the absorption of food or drink. No doubt a general decline in the subject's level of vitality can result in extreme cases, as we see for example in natural or artificial hibernation, but this is conceivable only as a phase that cannot last without leading to irreversible damage. The very reversibility of a neurotic problem implies that the economy of satisfactions that were involved in it were of a different order, and infinitely less tied to fixed organic rhythms, even if they command some of them. This defines the conceptual category that includes the sort of objects I am in the process of qualifying as imaginary, if you are willing to grant this term its full range of implications.

On this basis, it is easy to see that the order of imaginary satisfaction can be found only in the sexual realm.

All of this is but a precondition for analytic practice. And it is not astonishing, even if things had to be confirmed, verified, and inaugurated, I would say, by psychoanalytic practice itself. Once having gone through the experience of analysis, things seem to be perfectly rigorous. The term "libido" merely expresses the notion of reversibility that implies that there is a certain equivalence or metabolism of images. In order to be able to conceptualize this transformation, a term related to energy is necessary. This is the purpose served by the word "libido." What is involved is, naturally, something quite complex.

Imaginary satisfaction is obviously not the simple fact that Demetrius was satisfied by having dreamed that he possessed the courtesan priestess [Chrysis], even if this case is but a particular case in a larger whole. It involves an element that goes much further and that intersects all the phenomena that biologists mention concerning instinctual cycles, especially in the register of sexuality and reproduction.

Apart from the still uncertain and improbable studies concerning neurological relays in sexual cycles, which are hardly what is most solid in their studies, it has been demonstrated that these cycles in animals themselves depend upon a certain number of triggering mechanisms that are essentially imaginary in nature. What is most interesting in studies of instinctual cycles, their limits, and their definition is that, in testing a certain number of releasers to determine the lowest degree capable of producing an effect – in order to figure out exactly what these release mechanisms are – researchers have been able to provoke artificially in animals the activation of parts of the sexual behavioral cycle in question.

The fact is that, within a specific behavioral cycle, a certain number of displacements can always occur under certain conditions. Indeed, biologists have not found any better term than the very one that serves to designate the primal sexual troubles and mainsprings of symptoms in our patients: "displacement." For example, in the middle of a combat cycle, one can observe the swift supervening of a segment of display behavior. In birds, one of the combatants suddenly begins preening itself.

A thousand other examples could be given. I am not going to enumerate them here today. I am just trying to indicate that the element of displacement is an essential mainspring of the set of behaviors related to sexuality. No doubt, these phenomena do not occur in this realm alone. But the studies by Konrad Lorenz on the functions of images in the feeding cycle show that the imaginary plays just as eminent a role there as in the realm of sexual behavior. In man, it is principally at the latter level that we find ourselves faced with this phenomenon.

Let me punctuate this discussion by saying that the elements of displaced instinctual behavior displayed by animals can give us a rough idea of a symbolic behavior. What is called symbolic behavior in animals is the fact that a displaced segment of such behavior takes on a socialized value and serves the animal group as a marker for a certain collective behavior.

We thus posit that a behavior can become imaginary when its directedness toward images and its own value as an image for another subject make it capable of being displaced outside of the cycle that assures the satisfaction of a natural need. On this basis, neurotic behavior can be said to be elucidated at the level of instinctual economy.

As for knowing why it is always sexual behavior [that undergoes displacement], I need not return to this except to provide a brief indication. The fact that a man may ejaculate upon seeing a slipper does not surprise us, nor are we surprised when he uses it to bring his partner to feel better disposed toward him. But surely no one imagines that a slipper can serve to abate an individual's hunger pangs, even extreme ones. Similarly, what we deal with constantly is fantasies. During treatment, it is not uncommon that the patient or subject recounts a fantasy like that of performing fellatio on the analyst. Is that an element that we would characterize as an archaic cycle of his biography? Or relegate to a prior period of undernourishment? It is quite obvious that we wouldn't dream of such a thing, regardless of the incorporative character we attribute to such fantasies.

What does this mean? It can mean many things. In fact, we must realize that the imaginary can hardly be confused with the domain of what is analyzable. There may be another function than that of the imaginary. It is not because what is analyzable encounters the imaginary that the imaginary can be confused with the analyzable. The imaginary is neither the entirety of what can be analyzed nor of what is analyzed.

Let us return to the example of our fetishist, even if it is rather rare. If we accept that what is involved here is a sort of primitive perversion, it is not impossible to envision similar cases. Let us suppose it involves an imaginary displacement like the kind we find in the animal kingdom. Suppose, in other words, that the slipper here is a strict displacement of the female sexual organ, since fetishism is far more common among males. Were there nothing representing an elaboration on this primitive given, it would be as unanalyzable as is this or that perverse fixation.

Conversely, let us return to the case of the patient or subject in the grip of a fellatio fantasy. This is something that has a completely different meaning. We can no doubt consider that this fantasy represents the imaginary, a certain fixation on a primitive oral stage of sexuality, but we will not say that this fellatio performer is constitutionally a fellatio performer. By which I mean that the fantasy or imaginary element in question has merely a symbolic value that we must assess only as a function of the moment in the analysis at which it occurs. In effect, the fantasy does arise – even if the subject does not always tell us about it – and it does so frequently enough to show that it arises within the psychoanalytic dialogue. It is designed to be expressed, to be spoken, and to symbolize something – something that has a very different meaning depending on the moment in the dialogue at which it arises.

So what does this mean? First, it is not merely because a phenomenon represents a displacement – in other words, is inscribed in imaginary phenomena – that it is an analyzable phenomenon. Second, a phenomenon is analyzable only if it represents something other than itself.

2

To broach the topic I wish to speak about, namely, symbolism, I will say that a broad range of imaginary functions in analysis bear no other relation to the fantasmatic reality they manifest than the syllable "po" bears to the simply shaped vase it designates [in French, the *t* in *pot* (meaning pot or vase) is silent]. In "police" or "poltroon," the syllable "po" obviously has an entirely different value. One could use a vase to symbolize the syllable "po." In the term "police" or "poltroon," it would be necessary to add other equally imaginary terms that would not be taken for anything other than syllables designed to complete the word.

This is how we must understand the symbolic that is involved in psychoanalytic exchange. Whether it is a matter of real symptoms, bungled actions, or whatever we constantly find and refind, which Freud referred to as its essential reality, it is always a matter of symbols – symbols organized in language and which thus function on the basis of the link between the signifier and the signified, which is equivalent to the very structure of language.

The notion that a dream is a rebus comes from Freud, not from me. The fact that a symptom expresses something structured and organized like a language is sufficiently manifested by hysterical symptoms, to begin with the simplest of symptoms, which always provide something equivalent to a sexual activity, but never a univocal equivalent. On the contrary, they are always polyvalent, superimposed, overdetermined, and, indeed, constructed in the exact same way as images are constructed in dreams. We find here a coming together or superimposing of symbols that is as complex as a poetic phrase whose tone, structure, puns, rhythms, and sound are all crucial. Everything occurs on several levels and partakes of the order and register of language.

The importance of this will perhaps not sink in if we do not try to see what language is originally.

Of course, the question of the origin of language is a topic that can easily lend itself to organized, collective, or individual delusions. We must not engage in that sort of thing. Language exists. It is something that has emerged. Now that it has emerged, we shall never know either when or how it began, or how things were before it came into being.

But still, how can we express what is perhaps one of the most primitive forms of language? Consider passwords. I am choosing this example deliberately because the illusion, when we speak of language, is always to believe that its signification is what it designates. But this is not at all the case. Of course, it designates something, it serves a certain function at this level. But a password has the property of being chosen in a way that is thoroughly independent from its signification.

But what if the latter is idiotic? The Scholastics reply – one should no doubt never reply – that the signification of such a word is to designate the person who pronounces it as having such and such a property corresponding to the question that makes him pronounce the word. Others would say that it is a poor example because it is selected from within a convention. But this makes it even better. On the other hand, you cannot deny that a password has the most precious qualities, since it can help you avoid getting killed.

This is how we can consider language to have a function. Born among the ferocious animals that primitive men must have been – it's not unlikely, judging on the basis of modern men – a password is something thanks to which a group is constituted, not something thanks to which the men in a group are recognized.

There is another realm in which one can meditate upon the function of language: the stupid language of love. The latter consists – in the final spasm of ecstasy or, on the contrary, as part of the daily grind, depending on the individuals – in suddenly calling one's sexual partner by the name of a thoroughly ordinary vegetable or repugnant animal. This certainly borders on the question of the horror of anonymity. It is no accident that certain of these animal names or more or less totemic props are found anew in phobia. The two have something in common. The human subject is, as we shall see later, especially prone to vertigo, and to get rid of it he feels the need to create something transcendent. This is not insignificant in the origin of phobia.

In these two examples, language is particularly devoid of signification. We can clearly see here what distinguishes symbols from signs – namely, the interhuman function of symbols. This is something which is born with language and which is such that, after the word has truly become pronounced speech, the two partners are no longer what they were before. This is what words are for, as I've shown you now using the simplest examples.

You would, moreover, be wrong to believe that these are not fully fledged examples. Whether in the case of passwords or words of endearment, we are talking about something that is full-blown in scope. [Not so in the case of] a conversation that at an average moment of your career as a student you have at a dinner with equally average professors, where the signification of things exchanged has a character tantamount to that of conversations with people you meet on the street or the bus – nothing but a certain way of getting yourself recognized is involved here and this justifies Mallarmé's claim that language is "comparable to worn coins that are passed from hand to hand in silence."

Let us consider on this basis what happens when the neurotic comes in for an analysis.

He too begins to say things. We must not be surprised if, at the outset, the things he says have no more weight than the ones I just alluded to. Nevertheless, something is fundamentally different, which is that he comes to the analyst to exchange something other than idle chatter and banalities. Something not insignificant is already implied in this situation, since, in short, it is his own meaning that he has basically come to seek. Something is mystically placed here on the person who listens to him.

Of course, the neurotic advances toward this experience, this original pathway, with – by God – what he has at his disposal. What he believes first is that he must play the part of the doctor himself, he must inform the analyst. Naturally, in your everyday practice, you set him straight, saying that that's not what it's about, but to speak and preferably without seeking to put his thoughts in order or organize them – in other words, without putting himself, in accordance with a well-known narcissistic maneuver, in the place of his interlocutor.

In the end, the notion we have of the neurotic is that gagged speech lives in his very symptoms, speech in which a certain number, let us say, of transgressions with respect to a certain order are expressed, which, by themselves, loudly fustigate the cruel world in which they have been inscribed. Failing to realize the order of symbols in a living fashion, the subject realizes disorganized images for which these transgressions are substitutes.

This is what will initially get in the way of any true symbolic relationship.

What the subject expresses first when he speaks is the register of what we call resistances, which can only be interpreted as the fact of realizing an image or images of early experience *hic et nunc*, here and now, in the analytic situation with the analyst. The entire theory of resistance was built upon this, but only after the major recognition of the symbolic value of symptoms and of everything that can be analyzed.

Now, what psychoanalysis encounters is precisely something other than realizing symbols. It is the subject's temptation to constitute this imaginary reference point here and now in psychoanalytic experience.

We call this an attempt by the subject to draw the analyst into his game. This is what we see, for example, in the case of the Rat Man, when we perceive – quickly, but not immediately, and Freud doesn't either – that, by recounting the grand obsessional story of the rat torture, the subject attempts to realize here and now with Freud the very imaginary anal-sadistic relationship that makes the story piquant. Freud perceives quite astutely that something is involved that is translated and betrayed physiognomically on the subject's very face and that he qualifies as "*horror at a jouissance of his own of which he himself was unaware.*"

The moment at which people were able to gauge and posit as resistance elements that manifest themselves in psychoanalytic practice was certainly a significant moment in analytic history. This was first spoken about in a coherent fashion in Reich's article, one of the first articles on the topic published in the *International Journal of Psychoanalysis*, at the same time at which Freud constructed the second stage in the development of psychoanalytic theory, which is no other than the theory of the ego.

Around this time, in 1920, *das Es* [the id] appears. At that moment, we began to perceive, within the register of the symbolic relationship – and it must always be maintained there – that the subject resists and that this resistance is not a simple inertia opposed to the therapeutic movement, as in physics one could say that a mass resists acceleration. It establishes a certain bond that is opposed as such, like a human action, to the therapist's action, except that the therapist must not be misled by it. The patient is not opposing him as a real person [*réalité*], but rather as a certain image that the subject projects onto him, to the extent to which it is realized in his place.

These terms are, in fact, merely approximate.

The notion of an aggressive instinct is also born

at this moment, the term *destrudo* being added to libido, not without reason, for from the moment at which its goal [words missing here . . .] the essential functions of these imaginary relationships such as they appear in the form of resistance, another register appears that is linked to nothing less than the specific role played by the ego.

I will not go into the theory of the ego today except to say that, in any coherent and organized analytic notion of the ego, we must absolutely define the ego's imaginary function as the unity of the subject who is alienated from himself. The ego is something in which the subject cannot recognize himself at first except by alienating himself. He can thus only refind himself by abolishing the ego's *alter ego*. Here we see the development of the dimension that is already referred to as "aggressiveness," which is quite distinct from aggression.

We must now take up anew the question in the following two registers: speech and the imaginary.

Speech, as I showed you in an abbreviated form, plays the essential role of mediation. From the moment it is realized, mediation changes the two partners who find themselves in each other's presence. There is nothing to this that has not already been given to us in the semantic register of certain human groups. Read, in this regard, the book by Leenhardt entitled *Do Kamo*.

I wouldn't give it my highest recommendation, but it is expressive enough and quite approachable. It is an excellent introduction for those who need to be introduced to the topic. You will see therein that, among the Kanak people of New Caledonia, something rather peculiar occurs at the semantic level – namely, that the word "speech" signifies something that goes much further than what goes by that name for us. For them, speech is also an action. Note that it is for us too, for to give one's word is a kind of act. But, among the Kanaks, it is also sometimes an object – in other words, something that one carries, a sheaf [*gerbe*], for example. It can be anything. But, on this basis, something exists that did not exist before.

Another remark should also be made. This mediating speech is not purely and simply mediating at an elementary level. It allows two men to transcend the fundamental aggressive relation to the mirage of their semblable. It must be something else as well for, if one thinks about it, one

sees that not only does it constitute this mediation but it also constitutes reality itself.

This is quite obvious if you consider what is
called an elementary structure – in other words,
an archaic structure – of kinship. The structures
of kinship are not always elementary. Ours, for
example, are especially complex, but, in truth,
they would not exist without the system of words
that express them. And the fact is that the prohibi-
tions that regulate among us the human exchange
involved in marriage [*alliances*], in the strict sense
of the word, are reduced to an excessively small
number. This is why we tend to confuse terms
such as father, mother, son, and so on, with real
relationships. It is because the system of kinship
relations is extremely reduced, in its boundaries
and in its field. But it concerns symbols.

Jules H. Masserman published a very nice article in the *International Journal of Psychoanalysis* in
1944 entitled "Language, Behaviour and Dynamic
Psychiatry." One of the examples he gives there
shows clearly the weakness of the behaviorist
standpoint. Masserman believes he can resolve
the question of language's symbolism by pro-
viding an example of conditioning. Researchers
coordinated people's automatic reaction to light

– the contraction of the pupils – with the ringing of a bell. When they eliminated the light stimulus, the subjects' pupils would contract when the bell was rung. In a further step, the researchers managed to trigger the same reaction simply by having the subjects hear the word "contract." Do you believe this resolves the question of language and symbolization? If, instead of the word "contract," the researchers had enunciated some other word, they could have obtained exactly the same results. What is involved is not the conditioning of a phenomenon but what is involved in symptoms: the relationship between symptoms and the entire system of language, the significative system of interhuman relations as such.

Psychoanalysis precisely intersects these remarks and shows us their scope and presence in detail. The crux of what I just told you is in fact the following: any analyzable relationship – that is, any relationship that is symbolically interpretable – is always inscribed in a three-term relationship.

As we have already seen in the very structure of speech, what is libidinally realizable between two subjects requires mediation. This is what gives its true value to the fact, asserted by psychoanalytic theory and demonstrated by experience, that nothing can be interpreted in the end – for that is what is at stake – except via Oedipus. This means that every two-term relationship is already more or less marked as imaginary in style. In order for a relationship to take on its symbolic value, the mediation of a third personage is necessary who, in relation to the subject, realizes the transcendent element thanks to which his relation to the object can be sustained at a certain distance.

Between the imaginary relation and the symbolic relation lies the entire distance attributable to guilt. This is why, as psychoanalytic practice shows us, people always prefer guilt to anxiety.

Thanks to the progress made by Freud's doctrine and theory, we know that anxiety is always linked to a loss – in other words, to a transformation of the ego, to a two-term relationship that is on the verge of vanishing, and which must give way to something that the subject cannot approach without a certain vertigo. This is the register and nature of anxiety. As soon as a third party is introduced, as soon as it enters into the narcissistic relationship, the possibility of a real mediation opens up essentially by means of the personage who, in relation to the subject, represents a transcendent personage – in other words, an image of mastery by means of which the subject's desire and fulfillment can be symbolically realized. At this moment another register manifests itself which is either that of the law or that of guilt, depending on the register in which it is experienced.

3

You can tell that I am abbreviating things here a little bit. I hope it is not too disconcerting, however, since these are things that I have repeated many times in our meetings.

I would like to underscore once again an important point concerning the symbolic register.

As soon as the symbolic – that which is involved when the subject is engaged in a truly human relationship – is involved, as soon as a commitment is made by the subject that is expressed in the register of *I*, by an "I want" or "I love you," there is always something problematic. The temporal element must be considered, which raises a whole range of problems that must be dealt with parallel to the question of the relationship between the symbolic and the imaginary. The question of the temporal constitution of human action is inseparable from that of the relationship between the symbolic and the imaginary. Although I cannot discuss this topic fully this evening, I must at least indicate that we encounter it constantly in psychoanalysis and in the most concrete manner. Here too, in order to understand it, we must begin from a structural and, so to speak, existential notion of the signification of symbols.

One of what appears to be the most well-established points in psychoanalytic theory is that of automatism, so-called repetition automatism [or "repetition compulsion"], the first example of which Freud explained so clearly in *Beyond the Pleasure Principle* [(1920), SE XVIII, pp. 14–17]. We see there the first form of mastery in the making: the child abolishes his toy by making it disappear. This primitive repetition [i.e., making the toy disappear and reappear again and again] or temporal scansion is such that the identity of the object is maintained in both presence and absence.

This gives us the precise scope or signification of the symbol inasmuch as it is related to the object – in other words, to what is known as the concept. Now, something that seems so obscure when one reads about it in Hegel – namely, that the concept is time – is illustrated here. It would require a one-hour lecture to demonstrate that the concept is time. Curiously enough, Jean Hyppolite, in his [1941 French] translation of Hegel's *Phenomenology of Spirit*, confined himself to adding a footnote saying that this is one of the most obscure points in Hegel's theory. But, thanks to Freud's example, we can put our finger on the simple point which consists in saying that the symbol of the object is precisely the object that is here [*l'objet là*]. When it is no longer here, we have the object incarnated in its duration, separated from itself, and which, owing to this very fact, can be in some sense always present for you, always here, always at your disposal. This points to the relationship that exists between symbols and the fact that everything that is human is preserved as such. The more it is human, the more it is preserved from the shifting and decomposing aspect of natural processes. Man gives everything human that has lasted – himself first and foremost – a certain permanence.

Let me give another example. If I had wanted to broach the question of symbols from a different angle, instead of beginning from the word, speech, or small sheaf, I would have started from the tumulus over the chief's tomb, or over the tomb of anyone at all. What characterizes our species is precisely the fact of surrounding cadavers with something that constitutes a grave, marking the fact that this person lived. A tumulus or any other sign of burial warrants being called a "symbol." It is something humanizing. I term "symbol" everything whose phenomenology I have tried to demonstrate.

I obviously have my reasons for pointing this out to you. Indeed, Freud's theory had to go so far as to highlight the notion of a death instinct. The analysts who, afterward, stressed only the element of resistance – in other words, the elements of imaginary action in analysis, more or less canceling out the symbolic function of language – are the same ones for whom the death instinct is a notion that has no *raison d'être*.

To realize – in the strict sense of the word – to bring the image back to a certain reality [*réel*], after having included in it, of course, a particular sign of this reality [*réel*] as an essential function, to bring psychoanalytic expression back to reality [*réel*], is always correlated – among those who developed it in this register because they have nothing else – with bracketing or even excluding what Freud placed under the heading of the death instinct, which he essentially called repetition automatism.

Reich provides us with a typical example of this. For him, everything the patient recounts is *flatus vocis*, it's the way instinct manifests its armor. The point is significant and very important, but it is merely a stage in psychoanalytic practice. When the entire symbolic component of psychoanalytic practice is bracketed, the death instinct is itself excluded.

Of course, death as an element does not manifest itself only at the level of symbols. It also manifests itself in the narcissistic register. But there it concerns something else. Death in the narcissistic register is much closer to the element of final nullification that is linked to every type of displacement and about which one can conceive, as I already indicated, that it is the origin or source of the possibility of symbolically transacting reality [*réel*]. But it is also something that has much less to do with the element of duration, temporal projection, or the future as the essential term in symbolic behavior as such.

As you can tell, I must go a bit quickly over these things. There is much to say about all of them. The analysis of notions as different as those that correspond to the terms of resistance, transference resistance, transference as such, the distinction between what one should strictly call transference and what should be left to resistance, all of that can quite easily be theorized in terms of the fundamental notions of the symbolic and the imaginary.

In concluding today I would simply like to illustrate my remarks. One should always provide a little illustration for what one discusses. This is merely an approximation in relation to elements of formalization that I have developed much more extensively with my students in the Seminar – as regards, for example, the case of the Rat Man. It can be completely formalized with the help of elements like those that I will indicate to you. This will show you what I mean.

Here is how an analysis could, very schematically, be written from its beginning to its end.

$$rS–rI–iI–iR–iS–sS–SI–SR–rR–rS,$$

in other words, realizing symbols.

rS: This is the initial position. The analyst is a symbolic person as such, and he is sought out insofar as he is both a symbol of omnipotence and is already an authority or master. Seeking him out, the patient adopts a certain stance which is approximately as follows: "You're the one who possesses my truth." This stance is completely illusory, but it is the typical stance.

rI: Next, we have the realizing of images – that is, the more or less narcissistic instating in which the subject enters into a certain behavior that is analyzed as resistance. Why? Because of a certain relation [*rapport*], *iI*,

IMAGINATION

IMAGE

iI: This stands for captivation by images, which is essentially constitutive of all imaginary realization insofar as we consider it to be instinctual. The realizing of images is such that the female stickleback is captivated by the same colors as the male stickleback, and that they enter progressively into a certain dance which leads them you know where. What constitutes it in analytic practice? I am situating it for the time being in a circle. See further on [schema missing].

After that, we have iR, where I is transformed into R. This is the phase of resistance, negative transference, or even, in extreme cases, delusion that there is in the analysis. Some analysts tend to go ever further in this direction. "Analysis is a well-organized delusion," as I once heard one of my teachers say. This formulation is partially but not totally inaccurate.

What happens next? If the outcome is good, if the subject is not thoroughly disposed to becoming psychotic, in which case he remains at the stage iR, he moves on to iS, the imagining of symbols. He imagines symbols. We have a thousand examples of the imagining of symbols in analysis, for example, dreams. A dream is a symbolized image.

Here sS comes in, allowing for a reversal. It is the symbolizing of images – in other words, what is known as interpretation. One reaches it only after going beyond the imaginary phase which basically encompasses $rI–iI–iR–iS$. The elucidation of symptoms through interpretation now begins: $sS–SI$.

Next we have SR, which is, in short, the goal

of all health. The goal is not, as people believe, to adapt to a more or less well-defined or well-organized reality [*réel*], but to get one's own reality – that is, one's own desire – recognized. As I have emphasized many times, the goal is to get it recognized by one's semblables – in other words, to symbolize it.

At this point, we come to *rR*, which allows us to reach *rS* in the end – which is precisely where we began.

It cannot be otherwise, for, if analysis is humanly viable, it can only be circular. And an analysis can go through this same cycle several times.

iS is the analysis proper. It involves what is wrongly referred to as the communication of unconsciouses. The analyst must be able to understand the game his subject plays. He must understand that he himself is the male or female stickleback, depending on the kind of dance initiated by his subject.

sS stands for symbolizing symbols. The analyst is the one who must do that. It's not a problem for him as he himself is already a symbol. It is preferable that he do it thoroughly, with culture and intelligence. This is why it is preferable and even necessary that he have as complete a background as possible in cultural matters. The more he knows about them the better. sS must not come in until a certain stage has been reached.

The subject almost always forms a certain more or less successive unity whose essential element is constituted in the transference. And the analyst comes to symbolize the superego, which is the symbol of symbols. The superego is simply speech [*une parole*] that says nothing. The analyst has no problem symbolizing that speech, which is precisely what he does.

rR is the work the analyst does. It is improperly designated with the famous term "benevolent neutrality," about which people speak any old which way, and which simply means that, to an analyst, all realities are basically equivalent, all of them are realities. This stems from the idea that all that is real is rational and vice versa. This is what must give him the quality of "benevolence," upon which negative transference falls apart, and which allows him to bring the analysis safely to harbor.

All of this has been said a bit rapidly. I could have spoken to you of many other things. But it was merely an introduction, a preface to what

I will try to discuss more completely and more concretely in the report that I hope to deliver to you soon in Rome on the subject of language in psychoanalysis.

Discussion

Prof. Daniel Lagache thanks the lecturer and opens up the floor for discussion. Mrs. Marcus-Blajan indicates that she did not understand certain words, for example, "transcendent." What the speaker said about anxiety and guilt made her think of agoraphobia.

J. L. – Anxiety is tied to the narcissistic relationship. Mrs. Blajan has provided a very nice illustration of it with agoraphobia, for there is no more narcissistic phenomenon around. Every time I have commented on a case in my Seminar, I have always shown the different stages [*temps*] of the subject's reactions. In each case in which we find a two-stage phenomenon – in obsession, for example – the first stage is anxiety and the second is guilt, which provides relief from the anxiety in the form of guilt.

The word "transcendent" seemed obscure to you. It is nevertheless not a very metaphysical or even metapsychological term. I will try to illustrate it. What does it mean in the precise context in which I used it?

In the subject's relationship to his semblable – the two-term or narcissistic relationship – there is always something that has faded away. The subject feels that he is the other and that the other is him. This reciprocally defined subject is an essential stage in the constitution of the human subject. It is a stage in which he cannot subsist even though his structure is always on the verge of appearing, especially in certain neurotic structures. Where the specular image applies maximally, the subject is merely the reflection of himself. Hence his need to construct a point that constitutes something transcendent, which is precisely the other *qua* other.

A thousand examples could be offered. Let us consider that of phobia – that is, the fact that a similar anxiety corresponds to the subsistence in the human partner of animal images, which are quite foreign and separate from human images. In fact, whatever we may think of the real historical origin of totemism, and it is not transparent despite the studies that have been devoted to the topic, there is one thing that is quite certain, which is that totemism is linked to the prohibition of cannibalism – that is, the injunction not to eat the other. The most primitive form of human relationship is certainly the absorption of the substance of one's semblable. Here you can clearly see the function of totemism, which is to create a subject that transcends the semblable. I don't believe Dr. Gessain will contradict me here.

This intersects one of the points that interests you the most, the relationship between children and adults. To children, adults are transcendent insofar as they are initiated. What is rather curious is that children are no less transcendent to adults. By a system of reflection that is characteristic of all relations, a child becomes for an adult the subject of all mysteries. This is the source of the confusion of tongues between children and adults that we must take into account when treating children.

We could take other examples, in particular examples related to what constitutes the sexual type of Oedipal relations, which involves the subject in some way and yet simultaneously goes beyond him. We see there the constitution of a form at a certain distance.

Serge Leclaire – You spoke to us about the symbolic and the imaginary. But you didn't talk to us about the real.

J. L. – I did talk about it a little bit, nonetheless. The real is either totality or the vanished instant. In analytic practice, it always appears for the subject when he runs up against something, for example, the analyst's silence.

Through analytic dialogue, something quite striking occurs that I was not able to emphasize this evening. It is a facet of analytic experience that, in and of itself, would require far more than just one talk. Let me take an altogether concrete example, that of dreams, about which I no longer recall whether I said earlier that they are composed like a language. In analysis, they serve as a language. A dream that occurs in the middle or at the end of the analysis is part of the dialogue with the analyst. So how is it that these dreams – and many other things as well, [such as] the way in which the subject constitutes his symbols – bear the absolutely gripping mark of the reality of the analyst, namely, the analyst as a person, as he is constituted in his being? How is it possible that, through this imaginary and symbolic experience, the subject winds up in the final phase with a limited but striking knowledge of the analyst's structure? This in and of itself raises a problem that I was not able to broach this evening.

Georges Mauco – Perhaps we need to recall to mind the different types of symbols.

J. L. – A symbol is, in the first place, an emblem.

Georges Mauco – Symbols are lived experience. For example, a house is known first of all by a symbol, and is later elaborated and disciplined collectively. It always evokes the word "house."

J. L. – Let me say that I do not entirely agree. Ernest Jones has drawn up a little catalogue of the symbols that one finds at the roots of analytic experience – which constitute symptoms, the Oedipal relationship, etc. – and he demonstrates that what is at stake are always essentially themes related to kinship relations, the master's author-ity, and life and death. All of which obviously involve symbols. The latter are elements that have nothing whatsoever to do with reality. A being that is completely encaged in reality, like an animal, hasn't the slightest notion of them.

At stake here are precisely the points at which the symbol constitutes human reality, where it creates the human dimension Freud constantly emphasizes when he says that the obsessive neurotic always lives in the register of what involves the elements of greatest uncertainty: how long one's life will last, who one's biological father is, and so on. There is no direct perceptual proof of any of that in human reality. Such things are constructed and constructed primitively by certain symbolic relations that can then find confirmation in reality. A [child's] father is effectively its progenitor. But, before we can know who he is with certainty, the name of the father creates the function of the father.

I believe thus that symbols are not elaborations of sensations or of reality. What is properly symbolic – and the most primitive of symbols – introduces something else, something different into human reality, something that constitutes all the primitive objects of truth.

What is remarkable is that symbols, symbolizing

symbols, all fall under that heading. The creation of symbols accomplishes the introduction of a new reality into animal reality.

Georges Mauco – ... but sublimated and elaborated. This provides the foundation for later language.

J. L. – I completely agree with you there. For example, in order to designate relationships, logicians themselves quite naturally appeal to the term "kinship." It's the first model of a transitive relationship.

Octave Mannoni – The shift from anxiety to guilt seems related to the analytic situation itself. Anxiety can lead to shame and not to guilt. When anxiety evokes the idea not of a punisher but of being ostracized, it is shame that appears. Anxiety can also be translated into doubt instead of guilt. It seems to me that it is because the analyst is present that anxiety transforms into guilt.

J. L. – I quite agree with you. The analytic situation is unusual – the analyst [is felt by the patient to be the one who] possesses speech and judges – because the analysis is quite thoroughly oriented in a symbolic direction and because the analyst has substituted speech for what was missing there, because the father was merely a superego – in other words, a law without speech, inasmuch as this is constitutive of neurosis, inasmuch as neurosis is defined by transference. All of these definitions are equivalent. There are, in effect, infinite routings to the reaction of anxiety, and it is not out of the question that certain of them appear in psychoanalysis. Each one deserves to be analyzed in its own right.

The question of doubt is much closer to the symbolic constitution of reality. It is in some sense preliminary to it. If there is a position that one can essentially qualify as subjective, in the sense in which I mean it – in other words, that this is the position that constitutes the whole situation – it is clearly this one. When and how is it realized? That would require a whole separate discussion.

Wladimir Granoff raises a question regarding fetishism.

J. L. – Indeed, I did not come back to fetishism. The fetish is a transposition of the imaginary. It becomes a symbol.

A question is raised by Dr. Pidoux.

J. L. – Symbols are involved in even the slightest acting out.

Didier Anzieu – When Freud developed his clinical theory, he borrowed models from theories current at his time. I would like to know if those models come from the register of symbols or from the imaginary, and what origin should be given to them. As for the preliminary schema that you proposed today, are we talking about a change of models which would allow us to conceptualize clinical data adapted to cultural evolution or about something else?

J. L. – It is more adapted to the nature of things, if we consider that everything involved in analysis is of the nature of language – that is, in the final analysis, of the nature of a logic. This is what justifies the formalization I provided as a hypothesis.

As for what you said about Freud, I do not

agree that, regarding the subject of transference, he borrowed the atomistic, associationistic, or even mechanistic models of his era. What strikes me is the audacity with which he accepted love, purely and simply, as something not to be repudiated within the register of transference. He in no wise considered love to be an impossibility or a dead-end, something that goes beyond the bounds. He clearly saw that transference is the very realization of human relationships in their most elevated form, the realizing of symbols, which is there at the outset and which is also there at the end of all that.

The beginning and the end always involve transference. In the beginning, potentially: owing to the fact that the subject comes [to see us], the transference is there ready to be constituted. It is there right from the outset.

The fact that Freud included love in it is something that must clearly show us to what degree he gave symbolic relations their full range at the human level. Indeed, if we were to bestow a meaning on love – a borderline experience we can barely talk about – it would be the total conjunction of reality and symbols, which constitute one and the same thing.

Françoise Dolto – You say reality and symbols. What do you mean by reality?

J. L. – Let me provide an example. Giving someone a child as a gift is the very incarnation of love. For humans, a child is what is most real.

Françoise Dolto – When a child is born it symbolizes a gift. But there can also be a gift without a child. There can thus be speech without language.

J. L. – I am always willing to say it: symbols go beyond speech.

Françoise Dolto – We always arrive at the same question, "What is the real?" And we always manage to move away from it. There is another way in which to apprehend psychoanalytic reality than this one, which to my psychological sensibility seems quite extreme. But you are such an extraordinary teacher [*maître*] that we can follow you even if we only understand later.

Sensory apprehension is a register of reality, and it has a foundation that seems more sure to me, since it is prior to language. If there is no image of one's own body, everything occurs for the adult with the verbal expression of the imaginary. As soon as the other has ears, the subject cannot speak.

J. L. – Do you think a lot about the fact that others have ears?

Françoise Dolto – I don't, but children do. If I speak, it is because I know that there are ears to hear. Prior to the Oedipal stage, children speak even when there are no ears to hear. But after the Oedipal age one cannot speak if there are no ears around.

J. L. – What do you mean?

Françoise Dolto – In order to speak, there must be a mouth and ears. So a mouth remains.

J. L. – That is the imaginary.

Françoise Dolto – I met with a mute child yesterday who drew [a picture of a child with] eyes but no ears. As he is mute I said to him, "It's not surprising that the kid can't speak – he has no mouth." The child tried to draw a mouth with a crayon. But he placed it on the kid in a place that cut the kid's throat. He would lose his head, his intelligence, and his notion of a vertical body if he spoke. In order to speak, one must be sure that there is a mouth and that there are ears.

J. L. – That is all fine and good, but the very interesting facts you highlight are connected to something that was completely left aside, the constitution of the body image *qua* the ego's *Urbild*, and with this ambiguous knife-edge, the fragmented body. I'm not sure where you are going with this.

Françoise Dolto – Language is but one of the images. It is but one of the manifestations of the act of love, but one of the manifestations in which being, in the act of love, is fragmented. We are not complete since we need to be completed when we need speech. One does not know what one is saying – it is the other [who knows what one is saying], assuming the other hears one. What occurs through language can occur through many other means.

Octave Mannoni – Just one remark. Drawings are not images; they are objects. The question is whether an image is a symbol or a reality. This is extremely difficult.

J. L. – One of the most accessible ways by which one can approach the imaginary, at least in the phenomenology of intention, is by saying that the imaginary is everything that is artificially reproduced.

Introduction to the
Names-of-the-Father

I do not intend to engage in any theatrics. I will not wait until the end of class today to tell you that this first class of the Seminar is the last one I will give.

This will not come as a surprise to some of you who are abreast of what has been happening. It is for the others that I am making this announcement, out of respect for their presence here today.

I request that you remain absolutely silent during this class [*séance*].

Until very late last night when I received a bit of news, I believed that I would be giving you this year what I have been giving you for the past ten years.

My class today was prepared with the same care that I have always given it, week in and week out. I can think of nothing better to do than to give it to you as is, apologizing in advance for the fact that there will be nothing to follow it.

I

I announced that I would speak this year about the Names-of-the-Father.

It will not be possible for me to explain the plural in the course of this first exposé. At least you will get a glimpse at what I intended to contribute to a notion that I first laid out in the third year of my Seminar [*The Psychoses*, 1955–6] when I discussed the case of Schreber and the function of the Name-of-the-Father.

Since it is clear today that I will go no further, I will perhaps be more careful than I have ever been in pointing out the reference points in my past teaching that would have formed the general outline of this Seminar. I wanted this year to tie together for you the classes I gave on January 15, 22, and 29 and on February 5, 1958, concerning what I called the "paternal metaphor" [Seminar V, *Unconscious Formations*]; the class I gave on December 20, 1961, and those that followed in January 1962 concerning the function of proper names [Seminar IX, *Identification*]; and the classes from May 1961 on what is involved in the drama of the father in Claudel's trilogy [Seminar VIII, *Transference*].

The fact that I am pointing to my prior seminars for those who would like to try to surmise in what direction I intended to continue my discourse shows you that they blaze a trail that is already quite well structured, which would have allowed me to take the next step this year.

This next step follows from my Seminar on anxiety [*angoisse*, which can also be rendered as anguish or angst]. This is why I intended – and I will keep my promise – to show you in what way it was necessary to provide the outlines that I did in my teaching last year.

In the course of that Seminar [Seminar X, *Anxiety*], I was able to hammer home formulations like the following: "Anxiety is an affect of the subject." I did not put forward this formulation without relating it to structural functions that I have situated at length, especially that of the subject defined as the subject who speaks, who is grounded and determined in a signifying effect.

At what time – if I can say "time," but let us agree that this infernal term refers, for now, only to the synchronic level – at what time is this subject affected by anxiety? When anxious, the subject is affected, as I told you, by the Other's desire, *d(A)* here on the board. The subject is affected by that desire in an immediate manner, which cannot be dialectized. It is in this respect that anxiety is, among the subject's affects, the one that does not mislead [*ne trompe pas*].

In this "one that does not mislead" you can see sketched out the radical level – more radical than anything that has been derived from Freud's discourse – at which anxiety's function as a signal is situated. There is no way to situate its function as a signal if not at this level. This situating agrees with Freud's first formulations regarding anxiety as a direct transformation of libido, and so on. It is only by positing it in this way that those formulations remain comprehensible. Freud himself sensed this sufficiently to maintain them after writing *Inhibitions, Symptoms and Anxiety*.

Secondly, I argued against the psychologizing tradition that distinguishes fear from anxiety on the basis of its correlates, especially its correlates in reality, and the activities [*agissements*] it induces. I changed things here by saying that "anxiety is not without an object."

What is object *a*, whose fundamental forms you saw me trace out as far as I could take them? Object *a* is what fell away from the subject when anxious. It is the same object that I depicted as "the cause of desire."

What must operate by means of object *a* takes the place, for the subject, of the anxiety that does not mislead. This is what the function of action [*l'acte*] depends upon. I intended to spell this function out in the future. Nevertheless, I promise you that you won't miss it entirely since I have already discussed it in a book I'm writing that is due to be finished in six months.

I confined my attention last year to the function of object *a* in fantasy. It takes on the function there of propping up desire, insofar as desire is the most intense thing the subject attains at the level of consciousness, in his realization as a subject. This link confirms once again desire's dependence on the Other's desire.

I am tempted, at the moment of leaving you, to remind you of the radical, altogether restructuring character of the conceptions of both the subject and the object that I provide you with.

We have, of course, long since left behind every conception that would make the subject into a pure function of intelligence correlated with the intelligible [world], as in antiquity's *noûs*. Anxiety proves crucial here already. It's not that it can't be found in Aristotle's work, in the form of *agonia*, but for antiquity it can only have to do with a local *pathos* that subsides in the impassibility of the All. Aspects of antiquity's conception survive in what seems furthest from it – positivism – on which so-called psychological science was founded and still lives.

There is certainly something to the notion that there is a correspondence between intelligence and the intelligible. Psychology can show us that human intelligence, at its root, is nothing but animal intelligence, and this is not groundless. On the basis of the intelligible world, presupposed in the pregiven [*le donné*] and in the facts, we can deduce the progress of intelligence or its adaptation in the course of evolution, and even formally imagine that this progress occurs anew in each individual. It's all there – except that there is a hypothesis that is not even perceived by positivists, which is the hypothesis that facts are intelligible.

In the positivist perspective, intelligence is but one affect among others, based on the hypothesis of intelligibility. This justifies a psychology of Tarot card readers, which is concocted in places that are supposedly freest from this kind of claptrap: endowed university chairs. [To positivists,] affect, conversely, is thus merely an obscure form of intelligence.

What escapes people who study such teachings is the obscurantism to which they are subjected.

We know what it leads to: to the ever more intentional undertakings of a technocracy; to the psychological standardization of subjects who are seeking jobs; and to acceptance of the established boundaries of society as it currently exists, head bent forward under the [weighty] standard [*étalon*] of the psychologist.

I say that the meaning of Freud's discovery is radically opposed to that.

It was in order to convey this to you that the first steps of my teaching followed the way paved by Hegel's dialectic. This was necessary to create a breach in the so-called world of positivity.

Hegel's dialectic, when one considers it, essentially boils down to logical roots, as Hegel himself showed: to the intrinsic deficiency of a predicative logic. Which is to say that the universal, when closely examined – and this has not escaped contemporary logicism – can be founded only upon an aggregate [of things], whereas the particular, the only one considered to exist, appears to be contingent there. Hegel's entire dialectic is designed to fill this gap and to show, through a prestigious transmutation, how the universal can manage to be particularized through the path of scansion brought on by *Aufhebung* [sublation].

Nevertheless, regardless of the prestige of Hegel's dialectic – regardless of its effects via Marx, through whom it entered into the world, completing what Hegel signified, namely, the subversion of a political and social order founded on the *Ecclesia*, the Church – regardless of its success at this – regardless of the value of its political impact when realized, Hegel's dialectic is false. It is contradicted both by the evidence of the natural sciences and by the historical progress of the fundamental science – namely, mathematics.

Kierkegaard, who was alive while Hegel developed his system – which was at the time *the* System – just as immediately perceived, celebrated, and specified that in it anxiety is the sign or witness of an existential gap. I bear witness to the fact that Freud's doctrine is the one that clarifies this.

The structure of the relationship between anxiety and desire, [involving] a twofold gap between the subject and the object that has fallen away from him, where, beyond anxiety, he must find his instrument, the initial function of the lost object that Freud emphasizes – this fault line does not allow us to handle desire in the logician's immanence of violence as the only dimension that can force open logic's deadlocks.

Freud brings us back here to the heart of that upon which is founded what he thought of as illusion [in *The Future of an Illusion*]. As was done in his time – where diversion [*alibi*] was the rule – he called it religion. I call it the Church.

Freud advances with the light of reason onto the same field by which the Church, running counter to Hegel's revolution, remains intact and in all its modern-day splendor.

It is at the very root of the ecclesiastical tradition that Freud allows us to trace out a fork in the road that goes beyond, is infinitely deeper, and is more structural than the milestone he erected: the myth of the killing of the father.

It is here, on this shifting, oh so scabrous ground, that I wanted to make headway this year, not without flattering myself that I had in my audience ears worthy of hearing it – I'm speaking of representatives of the ecclesiastical order.

As far as the father is concerned – from their Father to the Church Fathers – they must allow me to say that I never found them sufficient.

Some of you know that I have been reading St. Augustine since I was an adolescent. Nevertheless, it was only much later, more or less ten years ago, that I became acquainted with his *De trinitate* [*On the Trinity*]. I opened it again recently only to be astonished at how little Augustine says about the Father. He manages, of course, to tell us about the Son, and quite a lot about the Holy Spirit. But one has, I will not say the illusion, rather the feeling that, when he writes, some kind of flight occurs, out of a sort of *automaton* [necessity], whenever the Father is concerned.

Yet Augustine is such a lucid thinker that I joyfully rediscovered his radical refusal to consider God to be *causa sui* [self-caused]. The concept is, indeed, totally absurd, but its absurdity can be demonstrated only against the backdrop of what I highlighted for you – namely, that there is no cause until after the emergence of desire, and that the cause of desire can in no wise be equated with the antinomic concept of being self-caused.

Augustine himself, who manages to formulate a notion that runs counter to all intellectual piety, capitulates nevertheless when he translates *Ehyeh asher ehyeh* – which I have long since taught you to read properly – as *Ego sum qui sum*, I am the one who is [*Je suis celui qui suis*, literally, I am the one who am], by which God asserts his identity with

64

Being. I intended to articulate for you this year all sorts of examples of other analogous formulations in the Hebrew texts, which would have shown just how off key and unwieldy Augustine's rendition is both in Latin and in French, even though he was a very good writer. This "I am the one who is," by which God asserts his identity with Being, leads to pure absurdity when it comes to the God who spoke to Moses in the burning bush.

2

I am thus going to recall briefly for you the meaning of the function of object *a* in its various forms – forms I spoke about last year. Those of you who attended my Seminar were able to see how far they went.

When the subject is anxious, little object *a* falls away. This fall happens early on [*est primitive*]. The variety of forms taken by the object that falls has a certain relationship to the mode in which the Other's desire is apprehended by the subject.

This is what explains the function of the oral object.

As I have stressed at length, its function can

only be understood if the object that is detached from the subject is introduced at that moment into the demand made to the Other, in the appeal to the mother, and traces out a beyond in which the mother's desire lies veiled. The act whereby a baby, who is in some sense astonished, tilts back his head, detaching himself from the breast, shows that it is only apparently that the breast belongs to the mother. It fundamentally belongs to him. Biology is instructive to us here: the breast is, in effect, part of the nutritive system, which is structured differently in other animal species. It has, in this case, a deeply rooted part and a part that is plastered onto the mother's thorax.

A second form of the object is the anal object that we know from the phenomenology of the gift, of the gift given when one is beside oneself [*dans l'émoi*]. An infant releasing its feces surrenders them to what appears for the first time as dominating the Other's demand, namely the Other's desire, which still remains ambiguous.

How is it possible that writers did not more clearly realize that this is the basis of so-called oblativity? The fact that psychoanalysts situated selfless giving [*oblativité*] at the level of the genital act can only be viewed as a veritable cover-up operation that reveals a true panicky flight in the face of anxiety.

On the contrary, it is at the genital level that Freud's teaching, and the teaching that maintains it, situates castration as a gap.

The psycho-physiologists who were Freud's contemporaries reduced orgasm to what they called the mechanism of detumescence, whereas Freud, right from the beginning of his teaching, articulated the aspect of orgasm that represents the exact same function as anxiety, as far as the subject is concerned. I felt it was important to demonstrate this to you last year. Orgasm is itself anxiety insofar as desire is forever separated from jouissance by a central fault line.

Don't object that there are moments of peace or fusion in a couple, in which each can say that he is well content with the other. We analysts look more closely and see how often there is, at such moments, a fundamental ruse [*alibi*] or phallic diversion [*alibi*] whereby a woman in some sense turns into [*se sublime dans*] a sheath, but whereby something that goes further remains infinitely outside. I have commented at length on the passage in Ovid in which the myth of Tiresias is forged in order to demonstrate this. The traces of the inviolate [*inentamé*] beyond related to feminine jouissance that we can see in the male myth of women's supposed masochism should also be mentioned.

I led you further still. Symmetrically – and as if on a line that is not redescending, but curved in relation to the summit where the desire/jouissance gap is situated at the genital level – I went so far as to highlight the function of object *a* at the level of the scopic drive.

Its essence is realized [in the scopic drive] in that, more than anywhere else, the subject is held captive by the function of desire. Here, the object is strange.

At this level, the object is, as a first approximation, the eye that in the Oedipal myth equates so well with the organ to be castrated. Yet that is not exactly what is at stake.

In the scopic drive, the subject encounters the world as a spectacle that possesses him. He is the victim there of a lure, by which what comes out of him and confronts him is not the true *a* but rather its complement: the specular image, *i(a)*. This is what appears to have fallen away from him. The subject is taken with the spectacle, rejoices in it, and is elated by it. This is what St.

Augustine points out and designates in such a sublime way – in a text that I would have liked to have you read along with me – as the concupiscence of the eyes. The subject believes he desires because he sees himself as desired, and he does not see that what the Other wants to wrest from him is his gaze.

The proof of this is what happens in the phenomenon of *Unheimlich* [the uncanny]. Whenever, through some incident brought about by the Other, the subject's image in the Other suddenly appears as if it were deprived of its gaze, all the links of the chain by which the subject is held captive in the scopic drive come undone and we witness the return of the most basic anxiety.

In the formula below, this anxiety is indicated by aleph. I had planned to introduce the sign with which to symbolize it today for the purposes of our work this year. Here is the aleph of anxiety:

$$(\underline{a} \lozenge \mathbb{S})$$
$$\aleph$$

This is what the relationship between the subject and little *a* looks like in its most fundamental structure.

I have not yet finished with the scopic drive, but I will pause to note the sort of step beyond that is being taken here and to expose, in a timely manner, the imposture involved in something that we analysts must know well – fantasy – which takes the form I articulated for you the year of my Seminar on transference [Seminar VIII, 1961–2] with the term *agalma*, the height of obscurity in which the subject is submerged in his relationship to desire.

Agalma is the object the subject believes his desire aims at and regarding which he most completely mistakes the object for the cause of desire. Such is Alcibiades' frenzy. Hence Socrates' retort to him: "Cultivate your soul" [*Alcibiades* 132c]. Which means, "Know that what you are pursuing is nothing other than what Plato will later turn into your soul – namely, your image. Realize that this object functions not as an aim but rather as a mortal cause, and grieve this object. It is merely your [own] image. Then you will know the pathways of your desire. For the only thing that I – Socrates, who knows nothing – know is the function of Eros."

This is how I led you to the door we are arriving at now, that of the fifth term for the function of little *a*, by which can be seen the range of the object in its pregenital relation to the demand of the post-genital Other, and its relation to the enigmatic desire whereby the Other is the locus of the decoy [*l'appeau*] in the form of *a*. In this fifth term, the *a* of the Other is, in short, the only witness that the locus of the Other is not simply the locus of mirages.

I did not name this object *a*, and yet, under other circumstances, I could have shown you its odd lighting during the last meeting of our Society, which concerned paranoia. I abstained from speaking about what was at stake – namely, the voice.

The Other's voice must be considered to be an essential object. Every analyst is required to give it its due and to follow up on its varied incarnations, both in the field of psychosis and, in the most normal of cases, in the formation of the superego. Many things will perhaps become clearer if we situate the source of the superego in object *a*.

A phenomenological approach allows us to begin to situate the [subject's] relationship to the Other's voice as an object that has fallen away from the Other, but we can only exhaust its structural function by investigating what the Other is as a subject. Indeed, if the voice is the product or object that has fallen away from the organ of speech, the Other is the locus in which "it speaks" [*ça parle*].

Here we can no longer escape a question: Beyond the one who speaks in the Other's locus – that is, the subject – what is there whose voice the subject assumes each time he speaks?

3

If Freud places the myth of the father at the center of his doctrine, it is clear that it is because of the inevitability of this question.

It is just as clear that, if the entire theory and praxis of psychoanalysis today seems to have stalled, it is because analysts have not dared to go further than Freud regarding this question.

This is why one of the people whom I trained as best I could spoke, in an article that is not at all lacking in merit, about "the question of the father." This formulation was bad and even gets things backwards, although one cannot reproach him for it. The question of the father cannot be raised because it is beyond what can be formulated as a question.

I would merely like to try to situate how today we could have sketched out an approach to the problem posed here.

It is clear that the Other cannot be confused with the subject who speaks in the locus of the Other, were it only through his voice. The Other, if it is what I say it is – that is, the locus where *it speaks* – can pose only one sort of problem, that of the subject *before the question.* Freud sensed this admirably.

Since after today I must fall silent, in a sense, I shall not fail to indicate to you that Conrad Stein, who is not one of my students, has blazed a trail in this field. If I weren't obliged to interrupt my Seminar, I would have enjoined you to read his paper. For it is sufficiently satisfactory to spare me the task of showing you how, despite the error and confusion of his time, Freud put his finger on what is worth keeping in the work of a number of authors – from William Robertson Smith to Andrew Lang – after the critique, undoubtedly founded from the specialist's vantage point, that was made of the function of totems by my friend Claude Lévi-Strauss.

Freud is living proof that someone who is at the level of the search for truth can surpass all the views of the specialists. For what would remain of their function – would there remain nothing other than *a* – since what must be at stake is the subject before the question?

Mythically [*mythiquement*] – which is what *mythique ment* [mythic lies] means – the father can only be an animal. The primal father is the father prior to the prohibition of incest, prior to the appearance of the Law – the order of marriage and kinship structures – in a word, prior to the appearance of culture. This is why Freud makes him into the head of the primal horde; his satisfaction, as in the animal myth, knows no bounds. The fact that Freud calls this father a totem takes on its full meaning in light of the progress brought by Lévi-Strauss's structuralist critique, which, as you know, highlights the totem's classificatory essence.

Thus we see that it is necessary to place after the totem – at the level of the father – a second term, which is a function that I believe I defined more extensively in one of my seminars than has ever been done before: the function of proper names.

A name, as I showed you, is a mark that is already open to reading – which is why it is read the same way in all languages – printed on something that may be a subject who will speak, but who will not necessarily speak at all. What proves this is that Bertrand Russell is mistaken here when he says that one could call a geometrical point on a blackboard "John." Russell may engage in some strange antics, not altogether lacking in value, for that matter, but it is quite clear that at no moment does he question a chalk point on a blackboard in the hope that said point replies.

I also mentioned the various Phoenician and other characters that Sir Flinders Petrie discovered in Upper Egypt on pottery dating back several centuries before the use of such characters as an alphabet in the Semitic region. This illustrates for you the fact that pottery never had the opportunity to speak in order to tell us that these characters are trademarks. Names are situated at this level.

Please excuse me, but I must proceed here a bit faster than I would have liked to under other circumstances. I am indicating to you the general direction to be followed. Let us now see what the path we are approaching brings us.

Can't we go beyond the name and the voice and take our bearings from what Freud's myth implies in the register that grows out of our progress, that of the three terms: jouissance, desire, and object?

It is clear that Freud finds in his myth a singular equilibrium between the Law and desire, a sort of co-conformity between them, if I can allow myself to double the prefix in this way, owing to the fact that they – each conjoined with and necessitated by the other in the law of incest – are born together. What are they born from? From the presupposition of the primal father's pure jouissance.

However, if this is supposed to give us the mark of the formation of desire in a normal child's development, mustn't we wonder why it gives rise to neurosis instead? I have emphasized this point at length for many years.

Here we see the value of the stress I allowed to be placed on the function of perversion as regards its relationship to the Other's desire as such. It represents the backing into a corner [*mur*] and the taking literally of the function of the Father or supreme Being. The eternal God taken to the letter, not of his jouissance that is always veiled and unfathomable, but of his desire as involved in the larger scheme of things – this is the core where, petrifying his anxiety, the pervert instates himself as such.

These are thus the two main arcatures. In the first are composed and combined so-called normal desire and the one that is posited at the same level, so-called perverse desire. This arch had to be posited first in order to display afterward the range of phenomena that run the gamut from neurosis to mysticism and to understand that what is involved here is a whole [structure].

Neurosis is inseparable in my eyes from a flight from the father's desire, for which the subject substitutes the father's demand.

In every tradition – except the one I will introduce where people are very uncomfortable with this – mysticism is a search, construction, ascetic practice, assumption, however you want to put it, a headlong plunge into the jouissance of God.

What we find traces of in Jewish mysticism, on the other hand, and then in Christian love and even more so in neurosis, is the impact of God's desire, which is pivotal here.

4

I am sorry to be unable to take these indications further, but I don't want to leave you today without having at least pronounced the name, the first name by which I wanted to introduce the specific impact of the Judeo-Christian tradition.

This tradition, in fact, is not that of the jouissance but of the desire of a God: the God of Moses.

It is before Him that, in the final analysis, Freud laid down his pen. But Freud's thinking surely went beyond what his pen transmitted to us.

The name of this God is but *The Name*, which is [Ha] Shem in Hebrew. As for the Name designated by the *Shem*, I would never have pronounced it in my Seminar this year for reasons that I would have explained, even though certain people know how to pronounce it. Moreover, there is no one single pronunciation, there are many – for example, those given to us by the Masorah – and they have varied over the centuries.

Besides, the property of this term is far better designated by the letters that enter into the composition of the Name and which are always certain letters chosen among the consonants. I studied some Hebrew last year with you in mind. The vacation I am giving you will spare you from making the same effort.

The *Elohim* who speaks in the burning bush [Exodus 3:2] – that we must conceive of as his body, *kavod*, which is translated by His glory [Exodus 16:7], but which, as I would have liked to explain to you, is something else altogether – what this God speaking to Moses tells him [in Exodus 3:14] is: "When you go to them you will tell them that my name is *Ehyeh asher ehyeh*. I am what I am [*Je suis ce que je suis*]."

Je suis [I am or I follow] – I am/follow the cortège. There is no other meaning to be granted to this "I am" than that of being the Name "I am." "But it is not by this Name," *Elohim* says to Moses, "that I made myself known to your ancestors" [Exodus 6:3]. This is what led us to the point at which I said we would begin the Seminar this year.

"God of Abraham, God of Isaac, God of Jacob, not of the philosophers and scientists," Pascal writes at the beginning of the "Memorial." One can say of the first what I gradually accustomed you to hearing – namely, that a God is encountered in the real. As every real is inaccessible, it is signaled by what does not mislead: anxiety.

The God who made himself known to Abraham, Isaac, and Jacob did so using a Name by which the *Elohim* in the burning bush calls him, which I have written on the blackboard. It is read as follows: *El Shaddai.*

אל שדי

The Greeks who translated the Septuagint were far more abreast of things than we are. They did not translate *Ehyeh asher ehyeh* [אֶהְיֶה אֲשֶׁר אֶהְיֶה, Exodus 3:14] by "I am Who I am," as St. Augustine did [*Ego sum qui sum*], but rather as "I am He who is" [or "I am the existing one"] – designating beings [*l'étant*], *Ego eimi ho on* [Ἐγώ εἰμι ὁ ὤν], "I am the Existent [*Je suis l'Etant*]" and not Being, *einai*. This is not correct, but at least it makes sense. Like the [ancient] Greeks, they thought of God as the supreme Existent. I = the Existent [*l'Etant*].

One cannot wrest people from their mental habits overnight. One thing, however, is certain: they did not translate *El Shaddai* as we do now by "the Almighty." They translated it prudently by *Theos*, which is the name they give everything they do not translate by Lord, *Kyrios* [or *Kurios*], which is reserved for the *Shem* – in other words, for the Name that I am not pronouncing.

What is *El Shaddai*? I didn't plan on telling you today, even if I were going to see you again next week, and I won't force open the doors, were they the doors of Hell, to tell you.

I intended to introduce what I could have told you by way of something essential – a rendezvous point with the aforementioned Kierkegaard – that in the Jewish tradition is called *Akedah*, "the binding": in other words, Abraham's sacrifice.

I would have presented Abraham's sacrifice in the form in which the tradition of painters has depicted it, in a culture where images are not at all prohibited. It is, moreover, very interesting to know why images are prohibited among the Jews, and why, from time to time, Christianity developed a feverish urge to dispose of them.

I will leave you these images, even if they are reduced to Epinal-type imagery [*l'image d'Epinal*]. Not to make up for my Seminar this year, for assuredly the Names are not there. But the images are sufficiently wide ranging for you to rediscover in them everything I have announced since the paternal metaphor.

Consider one of the two canvases that Caravaggio painted of Abraham's sacrifice. There is a boy whose head is pushed up against a small stone altar. The child is suffering and grimacing. Abraham's knife is raised above him. The angel is there – the presence of the one whose Name is not pronounced.

What is an angel? This is a question we won't have the opportunity to discuss together. But it would have amused me to tell you a funny story about my last exchange with Father Teilhard de Chardin.

"My father, how do you extirpate angels from the Bible with your ascent toward consciousness and everything that follows from it?" I thought I would end up making him cry.

"Come on – are you asking me this seriously?"

"Yes, my Father, I am taking into account the texts, especially the Scriptures, on which your faith is, in theory, based." With his namer of the planet, what could he possibly do with angels?

So here we see an angel who, whether he has Father Teilhard's consent or not, is restraining

Abraham's arm. Whatever the case may be regarding this angel, it is there for *El Shaddai*. This is the way it has always been seen traditionally. And this is what allows for the playing out of all the dramatic pathos Kierkegaard provides us [in *Fear and Trembling*]. For, after all, prior to the gesture that restrains him, Abraham went to this specific spot for a reason. God gave him a son and then gave him the order to bring that son to a mysterious meeting place. There the father bound him hand and foot, as one would bind a lamb, to sacrifice him.

Before we get all emotional, the way people usually do on such occasions, we might recall that sacrificing one's little boy to the neighborhood *Elohim* was quite common and not only at that particular point in time. It lasted for so long that the angel of the Name, or the prophet who speaks in the name of the Name, constantly had to stop the Israelites from beginning anew.

Let us look further. This son, you will tell me, is Abraham's only son. That isn't true. There is Ishmael, who is already 14 at the time. But it is true that Sarah had proven infertile up until the age of 90, which was why Ishmael's mother [Hagar] was a slave with whom Abraham slept.

The power of *El Shaddai* is demonstrated first by the fact that He is the one who is able to raise up Abraham from the milieu of his brothers and fathers. It is quite amusing, moreover, when one reads [the Bible] to notice, if you calculate the years, that many of them were still alive at this time. As Shem had had his children at the age of 30, and he lived 500 years, and throughout his lineage they had their children at around the age of 30, Shem was only about 400 when Isaac was born. Well, not everyone likes reading as I do.

Be that as it may, *El Shaddai* clearly played a role in the birth of this miraculous child. Sarah says so: "I am old and withered" [Genesis 18:12]. It is clear that menopause existed at the time. Isaac is thus a miraculous child, the child of the promise. We can easily grasp why Abraham is attached to him.

Sarah dies sometime afterward. At that point there are plenty of people around Abraham, and in particular Ishmael, who is there even though we don't know how to explain his presence. The patriarch is going to show himself as he is: a formidable sire. He marries another woman, Ketorah, and he has six children with her, if memory serves me well. But these children have not received the *berakah* [blessing] like the child of she [Sarah] who carried him in the name of *El Shaddai*.

El Shaddai is not the Almighty, for his power fades at the edge of his people's territory. When an *Elohim* who is on the side of the Moabites gives his subjects the proper ruse with which to push back their assailants, it works, and *El Shaddai* skedaddles along with the tribes that brought him along to the assault. *El Shaddai* is the one who chooses, who promises, and who creates through his name a certain alliance that is transmissible in only one way: by the paternal *berakah*. He is also the one who makes a woman wait until age 90 to have a son, and who makes people wait for still other things, as I would have shown you.

Don't reproach me for having been too flippant earlier regarding Abraham's sensitivity, for if you crack open a short book dating back to the end of the eleventh century by someone named Rashi – in other words, Rabbi Solomon Ben Isaac of Troyes, an Ashkenazi from France – you will find some strange commentary. When Abraham learns from the angel that he is not there to immolate Isaac, Rashi has him say, "Then what? If that's the way it is, have I come for nothing? I am going to give him at least a flesh wound, to draw a little blood. Will that please you, *Elohim*?" I didn't invent this – it comes from a very pious Jew, whose commentaries are highly esteemed in the Mishnah tradition.

So here we have a son and two fathers.

Is that all? Fortunately, the Epinal-type imagery, in the more sumptuous form of Caravaggio's canvases, reminds us that this is not all. There is one in which the ram is on the right and where you see the head that I introduced here last year, invisibly, in the form of the shofar – the ram's horn. This horn has indisputably been ripped off of him.

I will not have the opportunity to explore its symbolic value in depth for you, but I would like to end with what this ram is.

It is not true that an animal appears as a metaphor for the father in phobia. Phobia is merely the return of something earlier, as Freud said when speaking of totems. Totems mean that man – not especially proud to be such a latecomer to creation, the one that was made with mud, something that is said of no other being – seeks out some honorable ancestors for himself. We are still at the same point: as evolutionists we require an animal ancestor.

I won't tell you which passages I consulted whether in Rashi or in the Mishnah, namely in the *Pirke Aboth*, which are sentences, maxims, or chapters of the Fathers. I am mentioning the latter for those who might be interested in it. It is not as grand as the Talmud, as you can see for yourself since it has been translated into French. They are the only two references I wanted to give today.

Rashi expresses most succinctly that, according to the rabbinical tradition, the ram in question is the primal Ram. He was there, writes Rashi, right from the seven days of Creation, which designates the ram as what he is: an *Elohim*. Indeed, all the *Elohim* were there, not just the one whose Name is unpronounceable. The Ram is traditionally recognized as the ancestor of the line of Shem, the one who links Abraham, by a fairly short sequence, moreover, to the origins.

The ram has gotten his horns tangled in a thicket, which stopped him dead in his tracks [Genesis 22:13]. I would have liked to show you in the locus of this thicket something that has been commented upon at length elsewhere. The animal rushes into the sacrificial space, and it makes sense to emphasize what he comes to feed on so avidly, when the one whose Name is unpronounceable designates him to be sacrificed by Abraham in his son's stead. This ram is his eponymous ancestor, the God of his line.

Here we see the sharp divide between God's jouissance and what, in this tradition, is presented as His desire. The point is to diminish the importance of biological origin. This is the key to the mystery, in which can be seen the Judaic tradition's aversion to what we see everywhere else. The Hebrew tradition hates the practice of metaphysical/sexual rites which, during festivals, unite the community with God's jouissance. It highlights, on the contrary, the gap separating desire from jouissance.

Its symbol can be found in the same context, that of the relationship between *El Shaddai* and Abraham. It is there that the law of circumcision is primally born, making this little piece of severed flesh into the sign of the people's alliance with the desire of the one who chose them.

I led you last year, with several hieroglyphics testifying to the customs of the Egyptians, to the enigma of this little *a*. It is with the latter that I will leave you.

In concluding my remarks today, I will simply indicate that, although I am interrupting this Seminar, I am not doing so without apologizing to those who have been my faithful auditors for years.

There are, nevertheless, some among them who are now turning this mark against me, nourished with words and concepts that I taught them, instructed by ways and paths into which I led them.

In one of those confused debates in the course of which the group – our group – has shown itself truly, in its function as a group, buffeted about by blind whirlwinds, one of my students – I'm sorry to have to devalue his effort, which could surely have resonated and brought the discussion to an analytic level – thought he should say that the meaning of my teaching was that the true hold [*prise*] of the truth is that one can never grab hold of it.

What an incredible misunderstanding! At best, what childish impatience!

And I have people who are considered, I know not why, to be cultured among those who are the most immediately able to follow me!

Where has one ever seen a science, even a

mathematical science, in which one chapter does not refer to the next?

But does that justify us in believing truth has a metonymic function?

Don't you see that, as I have advanced, I have always approached a certain point of density one could not arrive at without the preceding steps?

Hearing such a retort, isn't one reminded of the attributes of infatuation and foolishness, the kind of garbage-dump thinking to which one is exposed when one works on editorial boards?

I have tried to enunciate how I seek out and grab hold of the praxis which is psychoanalysis. Its truth is in motion, deceptive, and slippery. Are you unable to understand that this is true because analytic praxis must move forward toward a conquest of the truth along the path of deception [*tromperie*]? Transference is nothing else – transference as what has no Name in the locus of the Other.

Freud's name has been becoming ever more inoperative for quite some time. If I advance progressively and even prudently, isn't it because I must encourage you not to succumb to the slippery slope analysis constantly threatens to slide down – namely, imposture?

I am not trying to defend myself here. I must nevertheless say that having, for the past two years, let others direct group politics in order to preserve the space and purity of what I have to say to you, I have never at any moment given you reason to believe that, to me, there was no difference between a yes and a no.

November 20, 1963

Bio-Bibliographical Information

The Symbolic, the Imaginary, and the Real

This is the original title. The lecture was taken down by a stenographer and then typed up. The text published here was established by me. I have indicated the one place in the text where a few words are missing – not many, it seems.

This was the first so-called scientific presentation of the new Société Française de Psychanalyse (French Psychoanalytic Society), which had just resulted from the split that occurred in the French psychoanalytic movement. The conflict would arise anew ten years later and lead then to Lacan's "excommunication" and the foundation by him of his own school, which he called the École Freudienne de Paris (the Freudian School of Paris).

Lacan drew inspiration for his triad from Claude Lévi-Strauss's article "The Effectiveness of Symbols" (published in 1949 and reprinted in 1963 in *Structural Anthropology*, New York: Basic Books), which proposes the succinct but wholly original definition of an unconscious that is empty, devoid of contents, a pure organ of the symbolic function, and that imposes structural laws on material composed of unarticulated elements coming from reality as from the reservoir of images accumulated by each person (see pp. 223–5). The concept of "individual myth" found in the same pages was taken up by Lacan in his 1952 lecture entitled "The Individual Myth of the Neurotic."

Following this lecture in July 1953, Lacan set about writing the report that he was to present in Rome two months later at the first congress of the new society and which was epoch-making ("The Function and Field of Speech and Language in Psychoanalysis," found in *Écrits: The First Complete Edition in English*, trans. B. Fink, H. Fink, and R. Grigg, New York and London:

W. W. Norton, 2006; see also the "Discours de Rome" (The Rome Discourse) in *Autres Écrits*, Paris: Seuil, 2001, pp. 133–64).

Lacan refers in the present lecture to the seminar he had just finished giving on the Rat Man as well as to the one he had given the year before on the Wolf Man. These seminars took place in his home in the rue de Lille and were not recorded by a stenographer. To the best of my knowledge, all that remains of them are some notes taken by those present. These two seminars thus could not figure on the list of seminars whose publication was foreseen and announced. In 1967, Lacan spoke of the seminar *On the Names-of-the-Father* as his thirteenth seminar (see below), thus including the two earlier ones, no doubt because superstition sees in the number thirteen a certain maleficent value and because, like Freud, Lacan had a predilection for numerology. Recall his article entitled "The Number Thirteen and the Logical Form of Suspicion" (*Autres Écrits*, pp. 85–99), which ends with an evocation of Judgment Day.

Introduction to the Names-of-the-Father

When I discovered the stenography of this class in the folder of *The Four Fundamental Concepts of Psychoanalysis* that Lacan had given me, I proposed to place it at the beginning of that Seminar, which was the first of his seminars to be published (in 1973). Lacan agreed, helped me establish the text, and then, at the last minute, changed his mind: no, the time had not yet come, he told me, for people to read this – it would be for later. He maintained this position up until his death, despite the case for publication that I made to him from time to time.

I note that I am publishing it shortly after the death of my own father, Dr. Jean Miller, who died on August 25, 2004, and who was buried in the Hebraic tradition in accordance with his wishes. Did I wish to make of this publication an homage to his memory or to be quite sure that he would not read it? The two are not incompatible.

Lacan begins his lecture by evoking the news he received "very late" the night before: he had just been struck off the list of training analysts of the French Psychoanalytic Society by the "education committee" of which he was a part. After years of sordid negotiations, his colleagues were informed they had to sacrifice him if they were to be recognized by the International Psychoanalytic Association as the official "French Study Group." Several months later Lacan referred to this as his "excommunication" (see the first class of Seminar XI, *The Four Fundamental Concepts of Psychoanalysis*, New York: W. W. Norton, 1978).

Lacan returned to the topic several times. I will merely mention here what he said in a lecture he gave in Naples in December 1967 ("La méprise du sujet supposé savoir" ["The Misunderstanding of the Subject Supposed to Know"], *Autres Écrits*, p. 337). Citing Pascal, as he did in the "Introduction to the Names-of-the-Father," he contrasted the God of the philosophers (in other words, the subject supposed to know) with the God of Abraham, Isaac, and Jacob (God-the-Father), and wrote: "The place of God-the-Father is the place that I designated as the Name-of-the-Father and that I proposed to illustrate in what would have been my thirteenth seminar (my eleventh at St. Anne Hospital), when a *passage à l'acte* by my psychoanalytic colleagues forced me to put an end to it after the very first class. I will never take up the theme again, seeing in this event a sign that the seal upon it cannot yet be broken for psychoanalysis."

A remark made by one of Lacan's students (J. B. Pontalis, who was at the time a member of the editorial committee of Jean-Paul Sartre's journal) is stigmatized at the end of the class. Lacan often came back to the statement Pontalis made, referring to it in the form: "Why doesn't he [he being Lacan] tell us the truth about the truth?"

JAM

Nota bene: Institutional documents related to this period were published for the first time in my two collections that are now out of print: *La scission de 1953* and *L'Excommunication*; others can be found in *Jacques Lacan & Co.: A History of Psychoanalysis in France, 1925–1985*, by Elizabeth Roudinesco (Chicago: University of Chicago Press, 1990).

Translator's Notes

I would like to thank Mario Beira, Matthew Baldwin, Rong-Bang Peng, and Héloïse Fink for their kind assistance on this translation. All errors here are my own.

The numbers in parentheses refer to the page and paragraph number of the present English edition.

The Symbolic, the Imaginary, and the Real

(5, 1)   *Le réel* (the real) and *la réalité* (reality) are often indistinguishable in ordinary French usage as well as in this stage of Lacan's work. When I do not translate *le réel* as "the real," I always put the French in brackets.

(5, 2)   In Strachey's rendering: "In his normal state he was kind, cheerful, and sensible – an enlightened and superior kind of person" (SE X, p. 248).

(9, 3)   Regarding Raymond de Saussure, see his "Present

Trends in Psychoanalysis," in *Actes du Congrès International de Psychiatrie* V (1950): 95–166.

(10, 4) The reference to Demetrius is to a novel by Pierre Louÿs entitled *Aphrodite*, published in 1896.

(13, 2) One should perhaps read: "nor are we surprised when a partner uses it to bring him to be better disposed toward her."

(16, 3) The term "rebus" seems to appear initially on the first page of chapter 6, "The Dream-Work," in Freud's *Interpretation of Dreams* (SE IV, p. 277).

(18, 2) *Répondre* (reply) also means "talk back" or give "backchat."

(19, 1) Regarding "calling one's sexual partner by the name of a thoroughly ordinary vegetable or repugnant animal," consider the French habit of calling loved ones by such names as *mon petit chou* (literally, my little cabbage, figuratively, my darling) or *mon petit crapaud* (literally, my little toad).

(20, 1) The reference to Mallarmé is to a passage in his preface to René Ghil (1866), *Traité du Verbe*; see Stéphane Mallarmé, *Oeuvres complètes*, Paris: Gallimard, 1945, pp. 368 and 857. Words are apparently missing in the stenography of this sentence and the exact meaning is thus uncertain.

(22, 3) See SE X, pp. 166–7. In Strachey's translation, the passage reads as follows: "his face took on a very strange, composite expression I could only interpret as one of *horror at pleasure of his own of which he himself was unaware.*"

(25, 1) Regarding Leenhardt, see "La parole qui dure" (Tradition, mythe, statut), *Do Kamo: la personne et le mythe dans le monde mélanésien*, Paris: Gallimard, 1947, pp. 173ff.

(25, 3) *Semblable* is often translated as "fellow man" or "counterpart," but in Lacan's usage it refers specifically to the mirroring of two imaginary others (*a* and *a'*) who *resemble* each other (or at least see themselves in each other). "Fellow man" corresponds well to the French *prochain*, points to man (not woman), the adult (not the child), and suggests fellowship, whereas in Lacan's work *semblable* evokes rivalry and jealousy first and foremost. "Counterpart" suggests parallel hierarchical structures within which the two people take on similar roles, that is, symbolic roles, as in "The Chief Financial Officer's counterpart in his company's foreign acquisition target was Mr. Juppé, the *Directeur financier*." I have revived the somewhat obsolete English "semblable" found, for example, in *Hamlet*, Act V, scene II, line 124: "his semblable is his mirror; and who else would trace him, his umbrage, nothing more."

(26, 2) A passage appears to be missing here, which could be roughly rendered as follows:

But if you live in a culture in which you cannot marry your seventh cousin because she is considered to be a parallel cousin or, conversely, a crossed cousin – or because she is in a certain homonymic relation to you that comes back every three or four generations – you would perceive that words and symbols play a decisive role in human reality and that words have exactly the meaning decreed by me. As Lewis Carroll has Humpty Dumpty reply admirably: "Because I am the master."

[The actual passage is as follows:

"But 'glory' doesn't mean 'a nice knock-down argument,'" Alice objected.

"When *I* use a word," Humpty Dumpty said in rather a scornful tone, "it means just what I choose it to mean – neither more nor less."

"The question is," said Alice, "whether you *can* make words mean so many different things."

"The question is," said Humpty Dumpty, "which is to be master – that's all."]

It should be clear to you that, at the outset, it is indeed man who gives meaning to words. And if words are then commonly agreed upon for the sake of communicability – namely, the same words come to serve to recognize the same thing – it is precisely due to relations, to an initial relationship, that allowed these people to be people who communicate. In other words, there is absolutely no question – except in a certain psychological perception – of trying to deduce how words stem from things and are successively and individually applied to them. Rather we must understand that it is within the total system of discourse – the universe of a specific language that involves, through a series of complementarities, a certain number of significations – that what there is to be signified, namely, things, must manage to find their place. This is how things have been constituted throughout history. And it is what renders particularly childish the whole theory of language that assumes we have to understand the role it plays in the formation of symbols. Such as the one given by Masserman . . .

(26, 3) Lacan discusses the paper by Masserman, found in *IJP* XXV, 1–2 (1944): 1–8, at length in *Écrits: The First Complete Edition in English*, trans. B. Fink, H. Fink, and R. Grigg, New York and London: W. W. Norton, 2006, pp. 225–7.

(31, 1) Colloquially, we might translate *l'objet là* as "this here object." It suggests "the object that is right in front of you." The French formulation imitates the translation into French of Heidegger's *Dasein* as *être-là*, literally "there being"; hence "there object" or "the object as present."

(31, 1) Reading *décomposant* (decomposing) instead of *décompensant* (decompensating).

(33, 2) The Latin *flatus vocis* means a mere name, word, or sound without a corresponding objective reality, and was used by nominalists to qualify universals.

(37, 3) Reading *analyse* (analysis) for *analyste* (analyst).

(41, 1) Reading *interdiction* (prohibition) instead of *interprétation* (interpretation).

(43, 5) The paper by Ernest Jones that Lacan refers to here was published in the *British Journal of Psychology* IX, 2 (October 1916): 181–229. It was republished in Jones, *Papers on Psycho-Analysis*, 5th edn, Boston: Beacon, 1961. See Lacan's "In Memory of Ernest Jones: On His Theory of Symbolism," in *Écrits*, pp. 585–601.

(51, 2) Regarding the *Urbild*, see "The Mirror Stage as Formative of the *I* Function," in *Écrits*, pp. 75–81.

(52, 2) A number of ill-recorded questions and responses are not included in this publication.

Introduction to the Names-of-the-Father

(56, 2)   In the French, this paragraph ends with a repetition: "and the class I gave on December 20, 1961, and those that followed in January 1962 concerning proper names."

(57, 4)   Or: "anxiety is, among the subject's affects, the one that is not deceptive"; "anxiety is something that is not misleading."

(61, 4)   Or: "can be founded only upon a negation."

(65, 1)   Augustine's "*Ego sum qui sum*" is sometimes rendered in English translations of his work as "I am Who I am" or "I am Who am." French grammar allows Lacan to say, "I am the one who am," whereas contemporary English grammar would require us to say, "I am the one who is."

       The New Revised Standard Version (NRSV), New International Version (NIV), and New American Standard Bible (NASB) all render the phrase from Exodus 3:14 as "I AM WHO I AM." In some of these versions there is a footnote raising the possibility of rendering the phrase as "I WILL BE WHO I WILL BE." On the other hand, the American Standard Version (ASV), following the King James Version (KJV), renders the phrase as "I AM THAT I AM." See the first full note on p. 104.

(66, 2)   *Dans l'émoi* could also be rendered as "when agitated" or "when highly emotional."

(66, 3)   A supposed tendency to give to others selflessly or disinterestedly, discussed in French analytic texts of the 1950s, translated here as "oblativity" (the adjectival form being "oblative"). The term was introduced by Laforgue in 1926 and was rendered as "self-sacrifice" in Lacan's "Some Reflections on the Ego," *IJP* XXXIV, 1 (1953): 17.

(67, 2) Or: "situates the gap constituted by castration."

(67, 3) Reading *orgasme* (orgasm) instead of *obstacle* (obstacle).

(68, 1) *Inentamé* could also be rendered here as "undiminished."

(72, 5) Jean Laplanche, *Hölderlin et la question du père*, Paris: Presses Universitaires de France, 1961. In English: *Hölderlin and the Question of the Father*, trans. Luke Carson, Victoria, BC: ELS Editions, 2008.

(78, 4) The Masorah (also written Masora, Massorah, and Massora) is a collection of critical and explanatory notes on the Hebrew text of the Old Testament, compiled from around the seventh to the tenth centuries AD and traditionally accepted as an authoritative exegetic guide, chiefly in matters of pronunciation and grammar. The masoretes were the ones who added vowel pointing to the originally consonantal Hebrew text, preserving the pronunciation of a language that was dying out in its living spoken form.

(79, 2) The New King James version translates the Hebrew here as "I am who I am"; other versions provide "I am that I am"; Rashi, like many others after him, renders it as "I will be what I will be."

(79, 3) *Je suis*, the first person singular of *être* (to be), is the same in French as the first person singular of *suivre* (to follow).

Exodus 6:3: "I appeared to Abraham, Isaac, and Jacob as God Almighty [El Shaddai], but I was not

known [or: did not make Myself known] to them by
My name YHWH." YHWH is the Tetragrammaton
often rendered, via the Hebrew periphrasis (or apo-
phasis) "Adonai," as Lord (*kurios* in Greek and
dominus in Latin). A later tradition, Jewish in origin,
was to pronounce YHWH apophatically as "Ha
Shem" (the name) when encountered in the text.

(80, 3) The Heideggerian terminology here, *l'étant*, can be
rendered as "beings" (as opposed to Being itself),
"entities," or "the existent."

(81, 5) *L'image d'Epinal*: Epinal images were popular prints
that told a story, and were often designed for people
who could not read. They provided a traditional,
naïve vision of things, showing only the positive side
of things. Figuratively, the term means "cliché."

(84, 1) Genesis 11:10 says that Shem begat Arphaxad (also
known as Arpachshad), Abraham's ancestor, at the
age of 100 and lived another 500 years *after* his birth,
making for a total lifespan of 600 years.

(90, 5) "Transference in what has no Name in the locus
of the Other" seems quite opaque; other versions
provide "*tant qu'il n'y a pas de nom au lieu de l'Autre,
inopérant*," which might be rendered as "as long as
there is no name in the locus of the Other, [that or
who is] inoperative."